THE BUSY WOMEN'S BIBLE STUDY SERIES

Embracing God: Trading Fear For Faith

A Four Week Study in the Book of Habakkuk

Mary Faassen

ISBN: 979-8-8432-9705-3

This study is first and foremost dedicated to my Lord and Savior, Jesus Christ! For without You, Lord, I would have nothing worthwhile to write about!!!

Forever, O Lord, Your Word is settled in heaven.
Psalm 119:89

Secondly, to my dear Husband Jon, who is my biggest supporter and encourager in following my passion to share God's Word with others. I love you, Jon, and I'm so thankful for you!

Table of Contents

An Introduction to "Embracing God: Trading Fear For Faith"

Hello Sisters, there are few things that excite me more than "sitting down with" other ladies of like mind and centering ourselves around God's Word! I can't tell you how blessed and honored I am to have you join me for the next four weeks! I only wish we were sitting at a table or in a study group, sipping on a cup of coffee and learning together in person! One day we will gather around Jesus' feet and fellowship with Him and one another. Until that day arrives I'm thankful we can still gather in spirit and learn His life-changing truth!

By way of introducing our study, please allow me to have a little fun by posing a multiple choice question! Please check all that apply. Ready? Here goes.....

*Who or what is Habakkuk?
—a character in Star Wars
—a minor prophet
—a province in the Middle East
—a Book of the Bible

If you noted that Habakkuk is a Book of the Bible you made an "A" for the day! Even better, if you checked "a minor prophet," you're batting a thousand! Habakkuk is both of these! But, I'm gonna be straight up and honest with you: Sometimes I fear offering a study on an Old Testament Book of the Bible, especially one most of us aren't quite so familiar with, might just cause us to want to look the other way. However, the very fact that you're holding this book in your hands proves you haven't scurried off just yet! I'm so thankful to you for coming onboard! I promise if you stick with it, you are going to relate to Habakkuk more than you could ever imagine! I will tell you the number one reason you are going to love this guy: Like you and me, Habakkuk was a fellow struggler. The short three chapter Book we will be studying affords us an up close and personal look into the life of this minor prophet, "warts" and all.

Let's just say if fear ever gets the best of you and you feel like you're shaking in your shoes, if the world around you seems to be spiraling out of control, (who hasn't felt like that lately?), or if you wrestle with questions of faith, Habakkuk is the guy you want to get to know. In the days ahead we will have the opportunity to do just that! Learning his story will encourage us in our own personal story that God is "writing" in our lives.

If Habakkuk could have borrowed a familiar cliche from modern day America, he might have exclaimed, "The struggle is real!" Things haven't really changed that much for us either. Many times we lament within ourselves just how hard this life can be.

Therefore, I can't wait to explore alongside you, this vital Old Testament Book! A hearty welcome to you! Again, I'm so excited you have chosen to be a part!

Week 1

Focal Passage:

Habakkuk 1:1-17

Week 1: Day 1

If you read the previous introduction to our study, you know by now Habakkuk is not a character in Stars Wars, although his name sounds like he could be. I'd like to give you a bit more of an introduction to not only the Book that bears his name, but also to the prophet himself.

Whether you're already familiar with him, or if this is your first time discovering Habakkuk's story, our time spent together in God's Word will better acquaint us with our protagonist. More importantly, my prayer is that it will move each of us closer to the heart of Jesus!!

Habakkuk is the 8th of the 12 minor prophets; "minor" signifying the length of their Books only, not their importance. This may be a short Book, but it is power packed and ever so relative to us today!

I'm reminded of what one of my friends shared with me years ago: She related that when she gets to heaven and meets some of the minor prophets like Joel, Amos, or "our own" Habakkuk, she didn't want to tell them that she knew nothing about their story because she had never taken the time to study it.

My friend was spot on: It's easy for us to stay away from the lesser known Books of the Bible and gravitate toward the more popular ones. Like my friend, I don't want to shy away from the smaller Old Testament Books, while missing out on what God wants to teach me from them.

With that being said, I think you just might "fall in love with Habakkuk." He's what I relate to most in a God follower: He loves his God, yet he is real; he has his share of struggles and questions. Still, he won't let go of the God who already has hold of him. In fact, Habakkuk's very name means "embrace!" Thus, the title for our study!

Through the prophet's fears, pain, and wrestlings, we will see faith winning out. As he embraces his God, we too, will be encouraged to embrace Him. And best of all, the same God Habakkuk encountered will have an encounter with us. As we open up His Word, He will reveal more of Himself to us! If you have a willing heart to know Him better, to overcome your fears, and see your faith flourish, pick up that Bible and let's jump right in!

*With a general introduction aside, please turn to the Book that bears the prophet's name and read Habakkuk 1:1-4.

We are no more than four verses into our study, and my guess is we can all relate to this prophet's inquiries and bewilderment over what is going on in his land. If I didn't know better I'd think Habakkuk had just watched our current evening newscast. Wouldn't you?

We see him asking "How long?" and "Why?" I don't know about you, but I feel an instant connection as I see this God-called follower voicing questions similar to the ones with which I struggle.

*Read back over verses 1-4 and record any connections you see to what is going on in our country today.

Scholars believe Habakkuk penned these writings in the mid-to-late 7th century BC. This would be not long before 586 BC, when the Babylonians besieged Jerusalem. The dates may have been way before our time, but as the old saying goes, "History repeats itself."

God knew when this Book was written, we who live in modern day America, would need to learn from Habakkuk's hardships. We can glean from the prophet how to live when our own nation appears to have spiraled totally out of control!

*How did Habakkuk describe what he saw in verse 1?

The prophet immediately relates the "burden" his own eyes are seeing. I'm reminded of a beach trip we took a few summers ago. Having stayed away from the news for a day or so as we soaked up the East coast sunshine, I was shocked to see what was happening in America once we got back to our condo and turned on the TV. It was deeply moving to see such desecration and disregard for our land through the intentional burning of a national city.

Such depravity and turmoil coming across the airwaves was overwhelming enough. Yet, Habakkuk, during the time he penned his own burden, was apparently much closer to his source of heartache. He couldn't turn off the television set, like I could. His problems were basically in his face. What dominated his thoughts was what he actually saw.....in the real! And it was bad!!!

It appears to the prophet that evil is winning: plundering, violence, strife, and destruction appeared to have ruled the day. Since my vacation I have watched via the airways more cities in my own country being torn apart. I can relate to Habakkuk's statement in verse 4: "the law is powerless, and justice never goes forth."

I told you we would relate to this Book of the Bible more than we could imagine. I would think, even worse than what Habakkuk was experiencing around him, was what was going on inside of him. We see a heart that is broken, crying out to God and wondering how long it would be before God responded to his earnest pleas.

Sisters, we are not alone! Many who have come before us, from Habakkuk's time, even before and after, have asked the same kind of questions. As we get ready to close out our first day of study, here's where it gets personal:

*Just between you and God, please complete one or both of the following statements:

-God, like Habakkuk, I am burdened for my country because____
_

-God, Habakkuk's burden was primarily for his country. Mine is a bit closer to home. It's what I'm experiencing in my own personal "world." Today I am burdened for________________________________

Habakkuk's openness and vulnerability to pour out his heart to God encourages us to do the same: As he is honest about his doubts and fears, we see that we can be, as well.

This brings us to our:

Week 1 Principle:

I ***embrace* God by taking my honest questions and doubts to Him!**

*Sharing Your Thoughts: Just from our Introduction and first day of study, how do you already see yourself relating to Habakkuk?

Week 1: Day 2

As we begin our second day of study, I was just thinking how nice it would be to grab a cup of coffee and sit down in person with each of you. I shared in our introduction how much I love fellowshipping with other Christian ladies! I'd love to hear your back story! I'd love to tell you mine. I'd love to hear what led you to this Bible study.......whether you've done several prior to this one, or if this is your very first.

Regardless of your answers to the previous questions, I simply love the way our great God works: Although we may not be meeting in a group together, He shows up and meets each one of us individually, right where we are!

I'm so thankful with all of my failures and inadequacies, God's Word is the one thing that reels me back in and keeps me on track! And I'm confident in knowing whatever our struggles may be at the moment, the Author of the Words we will be studying is with us and for us. May He bless you with an encounter with Himself today!

*For starters please glance back over the first four verses in Habakkuk.
-Now read Genesis 6:11.

-Remembering that Habakkuk most likely lived during the 7th century, what do the first four verses in Habakkuk, Genesis 6:11, and our current society all have in common?

Violence! We see it in movies and TV shows; it's depicted daily in our local, as well as, world news. It's important to remember Habakkuk didn't have any of our modern day technology to keep him in the loop. Like I mentioned yesterday when he said he "saw" this burden, I'm assuming his eyes actually beheld the violence and destruction amid his own countrymen.

Being called by God to share His truth, the prophet's heart must have been broken, knowing God's own chosen people had veered so far from Him. Sometimes we forget that when we are lamenting over the heartache around our world, or in our own personal "worlds," God sees it too.

Habakkuk was so sorrowful over what he saw going on around him, perhaps he too, had lost sight of the fact that God hadn't missed a thing. We can rest assured if unrighteousness and sin breaks our hearts, it must grieve our holy God so much more.

*How do the following verses relate the fact that God sees and knows all the grievous acts done on the earth?

-Genesis 6:5

-Jeremiah 16:17

-Hebrews 4:13 :

I don't know what it is about hurting, but somehow when we are experiencing great pain and angst we can feel like we have the monopoly on sorrow and heartbreak. And even worse, we can wrongly conclude since God is not stepping in to save the day, He must be immune to grief and sorrow. Nothing could be farther from the Truth. We are made in the image of God. Because He feels, we feel; because He hurts, we hurt.

*What does Ephesians 4:30 imply the Holy Spirit has the capacity to do?

Ladies, think about the last time you were truly grieved over the sin you encountered, whether it was your own or someone else's. Remember the depth of sadness that permeated your heart? Recall the exclusivity you felt at that moment, as you concluded no one else could understand the depth of your pain.

As you recapture in your mind that poignant experience, I want you to add another "picture" to the scene already in progress: Imagine Jesus right there in the midst of your hardship, carrying you in His arms and absorbing the brunt of your broken dreams and scarred heart. Because what touches us touches the heart of our God.

Habakkuk may have lost sight of this truth amid the chaos and confusion surrounding him, but God was with him during this dark time in Israel's history. He's with us during the political unrest that sweeps through our own nation. Like the prophet, we may wonder how long it will be before God intervenes. But God's track record is as follows: He's always on time and He always has a plan and purpose in our affliction.

Tomorrow we will see that God does indeed respond to His prophet's questions. And like Habakkuk, we might be quite surprised by God's reply.

*Sharing Your Thoughts: During the last time you felt great pain, did it occur to you that Jesus was right in the middle of the difficult situation with you? How does Isaiah 43:2 confirm this?

Week 1: Day 3

Have you ever asked a question and gotten an answer you totally didn't see coming? You know……that question you wish you had never asked, because you were in no way prepared for the answer? Well, I think it would be safe to say, if Habakkuk could pull up a chair, sit down and talk with us for a while, he could emphatically relate. Since that's not possible on this side of eternity, let's turn back to the Book of Habakkuk and rejoin the conversation between the prophet and his God.

*Please reacquaint yourself, one more time, with our beginning verses. What did Habakkuk inquire of God in 1:1-4?

-Read Habakkuk 1:5-11 to see how God answered His prophet.

God confidently and assuredly tells Habakkuk He is going to do a work in his days that the prophet would not believe. I like to send my daughters a text, or say to them in person, "I've got something to tell you that you are not going to believe!" It's an attention getter and sets them up to immediately want to know what it is that I am going to make them privy to. I confess sometimes I like to use a little mama drama!

I can't help but wonder in that split second between verse 5 and 6 that Habakkuk was holding on to hear some really, really good news……..like how God was going to "walk" right in and save Israel out of all the violence and pain they were experiencing. On the contrary, the prophet soon found out things were going to be far worse than he could have ever imagined. He certainly did not receive the reply he was hoping for.

Hmmmmmm!....God was making plans alright! He was raising up the Chaldeans to be the chastening rod for His wayward people, Israel. Say what? Can't you just see Habakkuk's hopeful countenance fall as God proceeded to describe this ruthless people group to him?

*Beside the following verses, list at least one bit of information you learn about the Chaldeans in Habakkuk Chapter 1.

-verse 6:

-verse 7:

-verse 8:

-verse 9:

-verse 10:

-verse 11:

Yikes! These descriptions would be enough to scare anyone! And worse than worse, these belligerent tyrants were going to be the form of dlscipline God would use to get His people's attention. It would be like saying someone like Hitler and his regime would be permitted by God to march through the United States, wrecking havoc as they go, with no regard to human life. They would be a way to chasten and discipline our country for its own sin. If I had heard that news, I would say to myself, "Run, Mary, run!"

Sometimes, as a nation, we get what we think we want. If we want to do things our way, apart from God, consequences follow. Israel had left the Love of their life, Jehovah, to follow after other "gods," doing what appealed to their flesh. This kind of desertion never ends well. God is merciful. He graciously calls His people to repentance. But when we, as individuals, or as a nation, do not heed His call, chastening awaits us.

*Have you ever been chastened on a personal level in order for God to bring you back to Him? If so, what did you learn from the experience?

-Please read Hebrews 12:6-11. How do these verses encourage us to be aware that even in times of discipline God's love for us never fails?

*Sharing Your Thoughts: Do you believe the current state of America is God's judgment on our land? Please explain your answer.

Week 1: Day 4

If we've never observed a back and forth dialogue between the Creator and one of His children, the Book of Habakkuk offers us a front row seat! You will recall from yesterday's lesson that God did indeed answer Habakkuk's queries, though it surely wasn't the answer the prophet was hoping for. I'm pretty sure most people don't exactly welcome impending doom. We would much rather see God's mercy and grace step in and change the hearts of His wayward children. Who wouldn't choose that, as opposed to being part of the mass suffering that comes to a nation that turns away from God?

We live in a day of easy-Christian-belief-ism (I may have just made that word up) where it is no longer popular to talk about God's wrath. We all want a God of love and mercy. As The Newboy's proclaimed in one of their earlier songs, "We want a God we can tame." A God of wrath confuses us and doesn't set well with our lax western worldview of Christianity.

Today we will veer away from reading in Habakkuk to explore the concept of God's wrath a bit more in depth. I know, I know!......Things are fixin to get a bit uncomfortable all up in here. But, Sisters, in order to truly grasp the depth of God's love, mercy, and grace, we must understand that He is also a God of wrath.

For if we don't, we have made God into an "idol" of our own opinions; we aren't fully embracing the God of the Bible. I promise Good News is coming before we end our study today!!! So, please hang tight with me! As the Book of James so courageously states, "God's mercy triumphs!" (James 2:13)

*Please read the following verses. Then write a sentence or two summation describing what you learned about God's wrath.

-Nahum 1:2

-Romans 1:18

-John 3:36

The previous verses are by no means an exhaustive list. Both the Old and New Testament speak to the wrath of God. Suffice it to say that to comprehend true salvation we must understand the fact that God hates sin: His wrath will come on those who reject His Son, Jesus,as the latter verse relates.

We could read after every great Biblical scholar and still come up wrestling with the concept of God's wrath and love co-existing. Mainly because, we are born sinners, and cannot comprehend completely the holiness and righteousness of God. He is in a league of His own, equal to no one!

We must accept the fact that God does indeed operate in wrath toward His enemies. To refuse to believe that truth is to reject portions of the Bible. God doesn't ask for our understanding, nor does He request our permission. He asks that we trust Him, even in the difficult concepts of theology that we find hard to grasp.

*How does Proverbs 3:5-6 confirm this idea?

Perhaps it will help us to remember that God's display of wrath is not akin to our displays of wrath. He doesn't just blow up one day and act ruthlessly, as if He is out of control. As one writer put it, "God's wrath is not an implacable blind rage……it is an entirely reasonable and willed response to offenses against His holiness."

God is faithful to always act in accordance with His character and truth. He always judges rightly because He alone is the Righteous Judge. It's also important to realize that God's wrath and love are intertwined. His unconditional love for us wants nothing but what is for our ultimate good. It is the highest love we will ever be afforded; a love that has a wrathful vengeance on the sin that can destroy us. Any act of wrath that comes from our holy

God is administered in wisdom and absolute righteousness.

Now here's the Good News I promised you!!!

*Please read the following verses. Which one speaks the most encouragement to you and why?

-Exodus 34:6

-Isaiah 30:18

-Romans 5:9

-1 Thessalonians 5:9

The ultimate wrath of God will come when He judges the world in its entirety. Thankfully, those who know Jesus Christ as their personal Lord and Savior, those who have repented of their sins and submitted to Christ's Lordship ARE NOT destined for that day of wrath. We ARE destined for a sin free, pain free, and joyful eternity with Him…. one that will never end!
A big, "HALLELUJAH and THANK YOU, JESUS!" goes right here!

*****(My friend, if you are not a Christian or are wrestling with the assurance of your salvation, please see the Appendix at the conclusion of this book.)

*Close out your day, thanking Jesus that He took God's wrath on Himself so that you could be forgiven of your sins. By His grace we will escape His ultimate wrath on the day of judgment!!!

Tomorrow, as we finish up our first week of study, we will be back into the God/Habakkuk dialog. You don't want to miss it. I love Habakkuk. Don't you? His transparency may just make us want to make him our new Bible study BFF! We will get to see just how real he is in tomorrow's lesson.

*Sharing Your Thoughts: Read the following quote and explain

how it balances out today's challenging concept:
"Do you wish to see God's love? Look at the cross!
Do you wish to see God's wrath? Look at the cross!" (From the Gospel Coalition.org)

Week 1: Day 5

Yesterday we temporarily veered off from the conversation between God and Habakkuk to consider the facet of God's wrath. As we recognized, there are concepts our finite minds will never be able to fathom; we must accept them by faith. I've heard it put this way, "God has a right to rule, and His rule is always right!"

If we could fully understand God we would be bringing Him down to our own mind's level. What a scary thought! Thankfully, instead, He calls us, by faith, to move our minds up and trust Him completely. Habakkuk received a lesson in this, and so must we. Again, let's turn to the pages of the Book that bears the prophet's name. Our Scripture passage today will contain his second question to God.

*Please read Habakkuk 1:12-17. If you had to condense Habakkuk's ideas in this passage into one main point what would it be?

There are so many things I love about verse 12. Most significantly is the fact that Habakkuk turned his thoughts away from the Chaldeans that God had just described in verse 11. The prophet refocused on his God!

Thus far we've recognized that like us, Habakkuk had his questions and his struggles. Just because he was God's prophet, he was not immuned to wrestling with his faith. As weak as Habakkuk may have felt after hearing God's declaration about the ruthless Chaldeans, he made the decision to focus on the Lord.....at least for a time.

Another thing I love about this passage is that Habakkuk used that tiny pronoun, "my," twice in verse 12. Please take a glance back at this verse. When fear and dread come assaulting us, we are wise to realize our God is near and personal to us. He is "my God" each and every day. He is yours, as well! So let's put into practice Habakkuk's example.

*Whatever is on your heart today, please write out a prayer of praise to God describing who He is to you. Like Habakkuk, personalize the pronoun "my" as you write. Be honest about your doubts and fears. He knows them anyway. Our close and personal God longs for us to be open with Him. He longs for us to know Him more intimately!

The next thing I love in verse 12 (Yes, we're still in verse 12) is when Habakkuk proclaims, "We shall not die."

A mental picture comes to mind. Once, when my daughter was young, she wanted to ride a kiddie version of the ferris wheel at Myrtle Beach. It happened as they were loading other children on the ride her seat stopped on the top. I saw my tiny little girl, in a seat all by herself, mouthing words into the air. When she got off the ride I asked her who she was talking to up there. On the tip top of that kiddie Ferris wheel, a bit scared and unsure, she told me she was telling herself she was going to make it through that scary ride. In other words, she was trying to convince herself she would be ok.

Perhaps, Habakkuk was doing the very same thing. As he was preparing for the scariest "ride" of his life, maybe he was trying to convince himself that he and his people would not die. He needed hope in order to face the future that loomed ahead of him, and so do we! These are "skeery" times, my friends!

*Here's a list of 5 things you can do when you need some convincing yourself:

1. Weather permitting, take a five or 10 minute walk outside; spend that time thanking God for His blessings, naming them specifically.

2. Memorize Hebrews 6:16-19

3. Every time you feel fear creeping in, speak a breathe prayer to God telling Him He is your hope! EVERY TIME your mind goes "south" you can choose to move it "north." This is called renewing our mind. It's a real battle some days, but it can be fought and won by turning our focus back to God and His Word..... time, after time, after time!

4. Call or connect with a Christian friend asking her to pray for you.

5. Start a gratitude journal, listing all the blessings God has given you.

As Habakkuk moves on with his lament, he voices his confusion to God as to how He can allow the wicked to "devour a person more righteous than he?" (verse 13) In other words, although the Israelites were living in sin, they weren't as godless as the Chaldeans; how could these wicked people be the ones used to discipline God's chosen nation? This takes us back to the age old question of why evil appears to be winning in this present world.

However, "present world" is the qualifier. In the here and now things will happen that we can't and don't understand. Sometimes evil will look like it's coming out on top. Sometimes the world will look like it's shaking and quaking around us, and we will question what the future holds.

But God hasn't called us to put our hope in this present world that can indeed be shaken. He has another goal for us.

*According to Hebrews 12:28 what are we receiving?

Don't you love it. Sisters? God's unshakable kingdom!!! What we are receiving is so much better than what we will one day be leaving behind! Habakkuk still had his feet placed on this earth's shifting sands when he penned these verses. Now he has moved on to a kingdom that cannot be shaken: He's in heaven; the place that awaits us, as well!

In light of the fact that we are on the journey to our ultimate home, we need to live out the latter part of Hebrews 12:28 in our daily lives: with a heart full of gratitude and a worshipful attitude of reverence and awe for the God of the unshakable kingdom.

As we close out this week I want to remind you of God's faithfulness to those who belong to Him! The world may be getting crazier, but we don't belong to this world; we belong to Jesus! The hardest trial of my life came in 2014. I taped the following verse to my computer as a reminder of God's promise in my greatest place of turmoil.

*Please consider writing out 2 Timothy 4:18 on an index card and remind yourself of it often. His faithfulness to you is steadfast and sure!!!!

*Sharing Your Thoughts:
What spoke to you most during your first week in the Book of Habakkuk?

****By way of review, please write out your *Week 1 Principle:*

Week 2

Focal Passage:

Habakkuk 2:1-4

Week 2: Day 1

Welcome back to study, Ladies! As we begin our second week together, I am once again in awe of God's timing in the narrative; it amazingly correlates to our present day concerns. Habakkuk may have been penned in the 7th century BC, but, as always, God's Word stands the test of time and is every bit as relevant to us today.

*Let's get started on our focal passage by reading Habakkuk 2:1-4.

*Please write the last line of verse 4 below:

We will revisit this passage next week; for the upcoming days we are going to take another little detour away from the Book of Habakkuk. I imagine by now you may have wondered how a three chapter Book was going to cover a four week study. Here's how……though we will deviate a bit from the main text, the theme will be the same. Habakkuk needed a refresher course on faith, and so might we.

Since "the just shall live by their faith," we sometimes need a reminder as to how God has called us to live on this side of eternity. Once we enter heaven and see Jesus face to face we won't need faith. But right now we do!

For the next five days we will invest some time in discovering what faith is, why it is so important, some common obstacles to our faith, and how our faith can grow.

*Please write out your own definition of faith below.

-According to Hebrews 11:1, what is the Biblical definition of faith?

-How does your definition resemble, or differ, from the preceding verse?

Someone has simply said, "Faith is taking God at His Word! And in case you haven't noticed, there is a lot of Word to take Him at: precisely 66 books, 31,102 verses, containing a multitude of promises.

Our Biblical definition of faith speaks of surety and confidence. It is believing that God is who He says He is and can do what He says He can do. Hebrews 11 not only explains what faith is, it depicts how it looks in the life of other believers. These folks struggled at times to trust Him, much like you and me. Chapter 11 is often referred to as the Hall of Faith.

*For your own personal study time today please choose one of the persons to which God has written His commentary on in Hebrews 11. Spend some time reading their personal story, as contained within this chapter. Then answer the following questions:

-Whom did you choose to read about in Hebrews 11?

-How did their particular story illustrate the faith they had in God?

-What was their story's outcome?

-How was your own faith challenged as you read their story?

***If you want to go a bit more in depth, you can do a Google search by finding the person you chose to read about in passages of the

Old Testament, drawing a cross reference on him or her.

The person's faith that amazes me the most is Abraham's. The testimony of this follower of God, offering up his son, Isaac, astounds me. (vs 17-19) As parents, we would do most anything to take the place of our child so that they would not have to suffer. It's almost impossible to imagine Abraham, after receiving his long awaited and promised son, Isaac, being willing to draw a knife to slay him in obedience to his Lord. Yet, Abraham did just that! God graciously intervened and provided a substitute ram for the offering.

*Verse 19 displays the depth of Abraham's faith. What did Abrham believe God could do?

At this point in Scripture no one had witnessed a resurrection. Yet, this faithful patriarch had experienced God giving him a son at the ripe old age of one hundred. His faith grew as a result of facing impossible odds, humanly speaking, of course. Abraham clung to God's promise that his seed would be blessed through Isaac, even as he grasped a knife and was ready to slay him. If God allowed him to follow through, he believed God would raise his son back to life. Now, that's some kind of faith!

This patriarch's story encourages me to believe no matter how things appear, no matter the challenges that come to test our faith, and regardless of the severity of our trial, nothing overrules God's promises in His Word. Aren't you so grateful for that?

As Hebrews 1:1 teaches us, through our great God we can be sure of what we hope for and confident of what we cannot see. Abraham's offering of Isaac is a picture of an even greater story. As we try to wrap our minds around how a father could give up his beloved son as an offering to God, we know God stepped in and provided a substitute for Isaac. However, God did not intervene by stopping the sacrifice of Jesus on our behalf.

The substitutionary ram in place of Isaac is a foreshadow of the substitutionary Lamb that was slain for us: The Lord Jesus Christ.

What love the Father has for His Son; yet what love the Father has for us that He did not stop the sacrifice Jesus was willlng to make on our behalf! Because He paid the price for our sin and became our substitute, we can live truly forgiven and free! Since faith is the topic of this week's study, let's introduce our weekly principle.

Week 2 Principle:

** We ***embrace*** God by choosing to walk by faith instead of by our feelings!**

*Close out your day by writing down what current circumstance challenges your faith the most. How can you approach your trial or concern with a greater measure of faith?

*Sharing Your Thoughts: How does seeing the faith of believers in Scripture, as well as those who are your contemporaries, encourage your walk of faith?

Week 2: Day 2

Today we will continue down the path of examining the reality of faith in our lives. Since we learn from the Book of Habakkuk that "the just shall live by his faith," we need to understand as much as possible what this directive means.

Let's look at two aspects of why faith is so important to God and why it should be to us, as well.

*Please read the verses below. Beside each one note the vital importance that faith has in our lives.

-Ephesians 2:8

-Hebrews 11:6

There are myriad passages of Scripture signifying how crucial faith is for us; in the previous two we see that faith is essential to our very salvation. It is also the avenue by which we please God. These passages describe our initial contact with faith as we become a believer, and subsequently, the way we continue to please God by believing Him in our everyday life. Faith, as seen in Ephesians 2:8 is the opposite of works. Yet we humans somehow think we can work our way into heaven.

*Give some thought to the following question and provide an explanation with your answer:

-Is it more difficult for you to believe you are saved by grace through faith in Jesus Christ alone?

OR

-Is it more challenging to believe your everyday Christian life pleases God when you walk by faith, instead of seeking to "do" works to earn His merits?

I love Jerry Bridges' insight on this matter of faith and works. He relates: "All of us have a natural drift toward a performance-based relationship with God. We know we're saved by grace through faith - not by works, but we somehow get the idea that we earn blessings by our works. After throwing overboard our works as a means to salvation, we want to drag them back on board as a means of maintaining favor with God."

*Does the former quote resonate with you or challenge you in any way?

Explain your answer.

Sisters, when we initially come to Christ for salvation we may have difficulty believing He really can forgive us of our sins. Yet, I suspect most of us that have been Christians for a while readily admit we're saved and forgiven by absolutely no merit of our own. We rely on God's grace and place our faith in Christ alone.

I wonder, however, if you all are anything like me? For a long time after coming to Jesus for salvation I still somehow thought I had to measure up. I wrongly believed if I had a good spiritual day, having read my Bible and prayed, (checking off my spiritual to-do list) if I needed God, my merits paved the way to His throne.

However, on the flip side of that coin, if I had not prayed and read my Bible, or I had lost my cool with my kids, or just felt like it was a bad day spiritually, I believed God was not really accessible if I needed Him. I wrongly assumed I had to work my way back into His good graces.

That kind of mindset does not please God because it is not of faith. What pleases Him is believing Him: believing Christ is my righteousness, believing I come to His throne on His merits, not my own.

Jesus is in the process of changing that mindset in me. Thankfully, it doesn't dominate me as it did before. Yet, I can still feel it creeping back into my theology, if I'm not careful. I have to keep reminding myself it is faith that pleases God. Certainly, I must come before Him and confess my sin and failures, but believing Him in faith also means I am only able to go before Him by His grace and no goodness of my own. When I repent of my sin, I am restored to fellowship with Him and do not have to do works of penance before I can feel I am back closer to my Savior!

How I long to grow in faith, to live moment by moment trusting Jesus! It's the only way to please Him! Living by faith is the only walk that affords us joy and freedom along the way!

*Please close out this lesson by talking to God about any areas in which you may struggle with the ideas presented today. Record any ways He is speaking to you during this time.

*Sharing Your Thoughts: How does 2 Corinthians 5:7 look when it is lived out in your life on a daily basis?

Week 2: Day 3

Sisters, today and tomorrow we will examine a few challenges we might find ourselves facing when it comes to our walk of faith.

*As we begin, please answer the following question: Has anyone ever told you that you were being presumptuous because you had absolute assurance that you were saved and going to heaven? If so, explain how you handled that encounter.

An obstacle to true saving faith can be the human understanding that declares, "It is prideful for a person to assume that he or she is good enough to go to heaven". I once had a lady share this same opinion with me. Her mindset apparently derived from a works based salvation. But, are our works ever really good enough to know we merit God's eternal heaven?

*How does 1 Corinthians 2:5 shed light on this Idea?

Once we really think about it, knowing with certainty that we are saved and will spend our eternity with Jesus is anything but prideful. For those of us who have been recipients of His grace, we know nothing we can do will ever be good enough to obtain our salvation. It's available to us by Christ's righteousness and His finished work on the cross on our behalf! Nothing more, nothing less. We, by faith, believe it and receive it.

It is necessary, however, for us to consider the connection between faith and works. In fact, the Protestant Reformer,

Martin Luther, took such issue with the Book of James that he questioned whether it really belonged in the canon of Scripture. Let's see why Luther held to this opinion in order to understand how faith and works can present a confusing issue.

*Please read James 2:14-26 carefully.

-Using one or two sentences, explain in your own words what James is conveying?

Luther believed this passage was contrary to the fact that the Book of Romans teaches us we are justified, or made right with God, by faith alone. (Rom. 5:1). Perhaps the reformer had the idea that James was trying to add works to salvation for it to be complete. There are, most likely, many people who believe this today.

*What about you? Do you believe a person is saved partly by their works? Explain your answer.

While this passage in James can be confusing if isolated and examined by itself, we must compare Scripture with Scripture.

*What does Ephesians 2:10 expressly state about our works?

There are other passages that hold a holy tension between faith and works. To sum it up in a nutshell, I believe James is telling his readers that when we have true saving faith, works will follow. We will love others, serve others, and most importantly, serve God. These will appear as works, yet, we are not working to get saved; we work because we are saved. That's a huge difference!

As Ephesians 2:10 relates, we are God's workmanship and

He has created us to do good works. Again, we do them with Christ working in our heart because we are saved! We don't do them in hopes that they will save us.

*Has looking at these two challenges in dealing with the issue of faith opened your eyes to anything new? Or has it helped you to understand these concepts better? Please explain your answer.

*Sharing Your Thoughts: How would you respond to someone who told you they believed you had to do good works to be saved?

Week 2: Day 4

One more considerable hindrance to our walk of faith can be summed up in one word: Feelings! Long about now I'm thinking of the 70's song by Morris Albert….. "Feelings, nothing more than feelings." I'm sorry if you are of a more youthful age and don't remember it! We girls who are a bit more up there in years probably remember its somber melody.

As women we are emotional and deeply feeling individuals. We love passionately, grieve intensely, and live devotedly; many times being fueled by our emotions. While feelings are not necessarily a bad thing, they can go south quickly if we allow them to negatively control us. As Lysa Terkurst wisely observes, " Feelings should be indicators, not dictators." I must admit I allow their dictatorship over myself quite often.

*When was the last time you allowed negative emotions to affect your attitude? Even ruin your day? What was the overall result?

If you are like me, you don't have to wear your brain out thinking too long or hard. Sometimes I can feel like a yo-yo; one minute I'm focused on Jesus with noble purposes to renew my mind; then the hands on the clock can move only slightly forward and I find I'm allowing a situation or circumstance to send me plummeting. Once again, I find myself in the grip of my treacherous emotions.

It happened to me just yesterday. I'm never happy with the outcome, and worse yet, I imagine Jesus is grieved when I allow my ever-changing emotions to control me.

As women, there are myriad emotions that we battle with; some of the most common are sorrow, anger, anxiety, jealousy, and fear.

*What dreaded emotion can you add to the list above?

We can allow our emotions to carry us off on an undesired path or we can acknowledge our feelings to God, yet still choose to walk by faith as we overcome their control.

*Look up the following verses. Beside each one identify the emotion, and note what God says about it.

-Psalm 34:18

-Ephesians 4:27

-Philippians. 4:6

-2 Timothy 1:7

After studying the previous passages of Scripture we recognize that while the feelings we experience are real, they can also be a REAL hindrance to our faith. We can choose to allow our emotions to drive us to God, or away from Him.

The good news is that when we choose to go to God with our heartbreak, anger, and every negative emotion we feel, we are taking steps in the right direction of faith. I love Oswald Chambers' short, but keen, observation: "We must battle through our moods and emotions." That's a simple statement packed with a lot of wisdom. It is freeing to know we have a choice to fight against the negative emotions and feelings that so easily drag us down! And God supplies us with the assurance we need for the fight!

*What does God promise us according to Romans 8:37?

Yesterday and today we've summed up some common hindrances to our faith. We must remember our fleshly self will always default to living by our feelings. However, we can learn to overcome the flesh by choosing to believe God's Truth and walk by faith!

I will conclude our lesson with one of my favorite quotes from Linda Dillow:

"God's Word is truer than anything I feel!"

*Sharing Your Thoughts: Today, how can you choose to walk by faith instead of by your feelings?

Week 2: Day 5

Now that we have explored what true saving faith is, why it is vitally important in our lives, and some of the obstacles or misconceptions we may have encountered in this area, we will consider some areas that will help grow our faith.

*Please read the following verses and note beside each one how our faith grows.

-Romans 10:17

-Luke 17:5

-James 1:22

-1 Peter 1:6-7

Hearing and reading the Word, asking God to increase our faith, acting on what God tells us in His Word, as well as the trials we go through, are avenues in which God produces spiritual growth in our walk of faith.

*From the previous paragraph, which "avenue" speaks to you the most, and why?

It is vitally important to hear God's Word read and taught through our local churches. If we are unable to attend church, the internet and television can be alternative ways we hear God's Word proclaimed. Another idea is that you can "hear" the Word by reading it aloud to yourself in your own personal Bible study time. You can also download a Bible app that reads the Word to you. ("YouVersion" is a great one to try). According to Romans 10:17 faith comes by hearing the Word of God! If we want to grow in faith this aspect is imperative.

In Luke 17:5 we get a glimpse of Jesus' disciple asking Him to increase their faith.

*Please read Luke 17:6. How does Jesus respond to the disciple's request?

Hmmm…….the disciples wanted a "bigger" faith but It seems Jesus is saying they don't need faith that's any bigger than the size of a mustard seed. Wonder what He meant? I think the answer is found in a quote my Sunday School teacher shared in class one day: "It's not about the size of our faith, it's about the size of our God."

When we pray for an increased faith, maybe we should also pray to better grasp the greatness and power of our almighty God!

As we continue to consider our growth in the faith department, James is quick to warn us that just hearing the Word, but not acting on it produces deception. Sometimes we can feel good about ourselves if we show up for church and even better if we get out our pen and paper to take notes. Though church attendance and writing down sermon notes is great, James would not be overly impressed. He implies God is pleased when we act on the truth we hear, read, and study. We should ask God to show us how to put into action what we are learning. Then we become doers of the Word!

We will finalize the context of our study today by observing the way trials work in our life of faith. This avenue is probably the one we would choose the least. Trials and hardships are not something we sign up for; yet they are an important way God proves our faith and enables it to grow.

*Think of the last trial you went through. Then answer the following questions.

-If you are still looking to Jesus and trusting Him, can you see that your faith was proven genuine through the trial? Explain your answer.

-How did your faith grow during the trial, or how has it grown since coming out of it?

It's amazing to me that the toughest hardships and storms I've faced have been the very times God has forged deeper roots of faith into the soil of my life. These challenges have shown me that when I've felt He was a million miles away, in reality, He had never left my side. And they have assured me that God is bigger, stronger, and more dependable than anything that has come my way. They have caused me to trust Him more! And isn't that what faith is all about? Though I still have a long way to go and grow, I'm thankful for a God that is going to see me through this life's trials and increase my faith along the way. And He's going to do the same for all those who keep looking to Him!

My sisters, we have veered off from the Book of Habakkuk this week to examine this life of faith that God calls us to walk (Hab. 2:4), but we should never veer off from the calling to walk it. It is our purpose, our peace, and our destiny until our faith becomes sight and we see Jesus face to face. It will be the one thing Satan tries to "kill, steal, and destroy," but the One who lives inside of us is far greater than our adversary! Praise be to Jesus Christ!

*Conclude by writing out 1 Timothy 6:12.

*Sharing Your Thoughts: What did you learn this week?

***Please write out your *Week 2 Principle:*

Week 3:

Focal Passage:

Habakkuk 2:1-20

Week 3: Day 1

Sisters, we're officially half way through our study! Thank you for your commitment to stick with it as we journey through this Old Testament Book! So far we've learned:

Week 1 Principle: We ***embrace*** God by taking our honest questions and doubts to Him.

Week 2 Principle: We ***embrace*** God by choosing to walk by faith instead of by our feelings.

Last week we studied the basics of faith; what it looks like and possible hindrances we may encounter. Today, we will be returning to Habakkuk's dialog with God, as the prophet's lesson in faith continues.

*Please read Hab 2:1-4. What, as recorded in verse 1, did Habakkuk purpose to do?

Watching and waiting on God is a challenge for all of us. No doubt it was a discipline in the prophet's life, as well. With all the technology and instant knowledge we have at our fingertips, we modern day Christians are challenged even further in the area of patience.

We have access to fast food, same-day deliveries, and just about "quick everything." I imagine our quest to watch and wait might be even harder for us in today's world than it was for Habakkuk.

*What do you have trouble waiting on in this season of your life? Do you think the personal challenge for you is more in the waiting or in the watching? Or do you think there's a difference? Explain your answer.

When waiting becomes long and tiresome it's extremely difficult to keep watching. Watching implies hope; a hope that continues to look to God, while trusting in His plan and His sovereignty. Sometimes it just seems easier to lose our hope than it is to fight to keep it.

We ended last week's study with encouragement and wisdom from the Apostle Paul: He told us to, "fight the good fight of faith." Hope is included in our fight for the faith! Our hope, our watching, once again, is to be focused on God alone!

*Please read the following verses and note what you learn about hope beside each one. ("hope" or "wait" may be used depending on your Bible translation)

-Romans 15:13

-Ephesians 1:18

-Psalm 33:18

-Isaiah 40:31

*Glancing back at Isaiah 40:31, what exactly does this verse tell us to wait on?

I remember learning in a previous study that we automatically are waiting on the thing we want God to do. We easily get discouraged when we don't see Him doing it, especially within our time frame. Isaiah seems to imply it's not the thing we want to see God do that we are to wait on, it's the Lord Himself!

*How is waiting on a thing and waiting on the Lord different? Give this some thought before you explain your answer.

When we wait on the Lord, we are engaging in the most important relationship we will ever have. Instead of just waiting on God to do something for us, we are waiting on our Lord, Himself. And when we wait on Him, He will reveal more of Himself to us. During the challenging process of waiting, we will come to know Him better.

Selwyn Hughes says it like this: "Whatever gets our attention, gets us." God had gotten Habakkuk's attention; we see the prophet stationing himself as he watches patiently. All the while God is "getting" Habakkuk; drawing him to become a man of deep faith. And faith is oftentimes forged in the waiting. I want to be a woman with a strong faith, don't you? So, Sisters, we must learn to wait on the Lord!

This week we will look at some other hindrances to our walk of faith, while remaining primarily in the Book of Habakkuk. This brings us to our Week 3 principle.

Week 3 Principle:

We ***embrace* God when we choose to turn from our pride and from idols to wait on Him.**

*Sharing Your Thoughts: What is your biggest challenge while waiting on the Lord?

Week 3: Day 2

We're going to jump right in on our focal passage today, Ladies!

*Please read Habakkuk 2:4-7 using the NKJV if possible. Because we explored what the walk of faith looks like in Week 2, we won't camp out on verse 4 today. I did want you to read it again in order to see it in context with verses 5-7.

*How would you sum up verses 5-7 in one sentence?

*One more time, please scan back over verse 4, connecting it with verse 5. What word do you see used in both verses that describe the soul of the unrighteous person?

Proud/Pride!......those two ugly words that keep relationships from being restored, that hinders us from admitting that we are wrong, and worst of all, can keep a person from turning their life over to Christ. Also, one of the most hideous things about pride is the fact that I can easily spot it in the lives of others, yet fail to recognize it when it raises its ugly head in me.

*What about you? Without naming names, how have you seen pride dominating someone else's life? Thinking over the last week, can you recognize any signs of pride dictating your thoughts and actions?

*Please read Romans 12:3 & 16. Keeping in mind Paul was writing these verses to Christians, what were his basic instructions concerning pride?

*Before we close out today, take a few minutes to do a google search of the word proud/pride in the Bible. Note any verses that seem to speak directly to you.

We can quickly acknowledge that God's Word has much to say about pride. We also must admit we struggle with it on a daily basis. For pride is an ugly assailant that easily asserts itself, even in the life of believers.

Tomorrow we will look more into pride's origin and its devastating effects in our lives. Finish up today by pondering the following story:

"John Bunyan, a famous Puritan preacher of the 1600's, was said to have been approached by a man following one of his sermons. The congregate told Bunyan what a fine sermon he preached; to which the preacher replied: "You're too late. The devil told me the same thing before I stepped down from the pulpit."

*Sharing Your Thoughts: What is the most destructive thing you have seen pride do?

Week 3: Day 3

*As we continue in our study today we will observe God's commentary on those who are His enemies. Please read Habakkuk 2:8-12. Though the word proud/pride is not mentioned in these verses, look at them again carefully. Do you see any evidence of pride operating in the people group described here.

-List your findings below.

Among the many and varied forms of pride, verse 9 asserts that greed is one of them. Left to themselves, people who have a lot typically want more. But even those who have very little, can be lured into greed. It's not so much about what you have or don't have, it's the attitude of the heart that matters.

*Why do you think greed is associated with pride?

*Read the following verses, sharing what you learn.

-Ecclesiastes 5:10

-Hebrews 13:5

-Luke 12:15

-Matthew 6:24

Pride and greed are horrific offenses against God.

Their very nature is rooted in independence from God.
Pride and greed find their origin in Satan.

*Please read Isaiah 14:12-15. This passage is believed by scholars to be pertaining to the king of Babylon, as well as to Satan.

-Count how many times the subject in these verses is using the word "I". It's been observed that there is an "I" right smack dab in the middle of the word, "pride." Something to ponder, isn't it?

As we've learned the past couple of days, pride is something that can take hold of God's children. It's connected with greed, because greed says we deserve more than God has given us; pride lures us to a sense of entitlement.

As long as we live on this earth there will always be someone more wealthy, more successful, and more popular than we are. If we keep our focus on them we will allow greed and envy to enter our hearts. It's the total opposite with Jesus Christ. If we keep our gaze on Him we will recognize He gives us all that we need. In Him we find the true "secret" of contentment.

*How does the description of Jesus in Philippians 2:7-8 completely counter the mindset of Satan in the previous verses from Isaiah?

*Sharing Your Thoughts: How can the truth of 1 Timothy 6:6-8 help keep the monster of pride and greed from wreaking havoc in your life?

Week 3: Day 4

Ladies, yesterday we looked at the connection between pride and greed. We recognized that God, from our passages in Habakkuk, is referring to the identification of the wicked who do not know Him. However, as we've observed, Christians are far from immune to the lure of pride and greed in their lives.

*By way of review, and to connect us to today's reading, please take a minute to brainstorm and list a couple of ways pride could be exhibited in the life of a Christ follower.

I'm quickly reminded of the times I've taught Bible study and secretly hoped someone would give me a pat on the back for it. Another thought comes to mind: The times my children have not responded in a Christ-like manner in front of other people and I'm embarrassed by what others will think of me. Pride can rear its ugly head easily in the life of a people pleaser, and I know me enough to know I can descend into this trap. Thankfully there's an antidote to pride. If we look closely we can see it in today's text.

*Please read Habakkuk 2:13-17. Keying in on verse 14, how can this passage lend help to those of us who want to live Christlike and overcome the ugly monster of pride?

There is coming a day when God's glory will fill the entire earth. But for now, those of us who know Him, are to live for His glory while on this earth..

*Read the following verses and note what you learn about God's glory.

-Isaiah 42:8

-Jeremiah 9:23-24 ("glory" may be translated "boast" in some versions)

-2 Corinthians 4:6

Although there are myriad verses on God's glory, from just the previous three we can discern:

- Only God is worthy of glory; no one is His equal.
- We, as recipients of His love, grace, and mercy, are to boast or glory in Him alone.

The same all powerful God, who created light at the dawn of creation, has just as powerfully shone His light of redemption into our hearts at the moment of our salvation. We get to know this glorious God in the person of Jesus Christ.

So how does this fit into today's reading? Glance back over verses 13-17. Notice that what God is characterizing here is the nature of man without God. Although these ruthless Chaldeans would be the avenue God would use to bring judgment on His chosen nation, they too, would experience His judgment in God's perfect timing.

As I read over these verses I see drunkenness, immorality, shame, and violence described among the enemies of God. We may be in a completely different era, but man apart from God never really changes. Turn on your TV and the same areas of sin will be depicted on the screen before you.

God had called His man, Habakkuk, to live a God honoring life in the midst of corruptness all around him. Likewise, He calls us, His women, to do the same. We can't stand well for Christ if we blend in with the culture.

*What is God's admonition to us in 2 Corinthians 6:17?

-How can we affect the culture for Christ, without being drawn into it?

-Prayerfully ask God to show you anything He may want you to give up so that you can draw closer to Him, living more Christ-like before unbelievers.

*Sharing Your Thoughts: Today we read 2 Corinthians 4:6, which refers to the time when God shone His light into our hearts and we became His. Briefly share your salvation date or a testimony of the difference He has made in your life! (Let the redeemed of the Lord say so! Psalm 107:2a)

Week 3: Day 5

Ladies, today we will wrap up our week of study, leaving us with only one week to go. Before we turn to our Scripture reading, please answer the following question.

*What do you feel stands out to you the most at this point in our study, and how can you apply it in your everyday life?

*Please turn to Habakkuk 2:18-20 as we finish out Chapter 2. What is the general topic of these three verses?

God is relating to us the futility of serving idols. We, in modern day America, are not too familiar with carved idols, or are we? Several years ago I heard a real estate agent say she worked amid contemporaries who would bury a carved statue upside down, believing this would help their real estate sales.

This reminds me of what we've already observed in our study: people haven't really changed much over the years; men's depravity pretty much continues to look the same.

*Please go back to verses 18 and 19 and jot down everything you learn about idols?

It's easy to recognize idol worship in non-believers when they bow before a carving or molded image. The Bible is full of examples of such worship. Yet, similar to the area of pride, idol worship can be harder to discern in the life of a believer. Still, we can find it within our own hearts.

*Consider the following:

-a person is so caught up in their work they neglect God's House and their family to climb up the corporate ladder

-a woman is unable to have children and holds on to anger and jealousy toward those who can, along with anger toward God

-a person neglects giving their tithe and ministering to others monetarily in order to accumulate more wealth for themselves

-a person is jealous over another's talents, wealth, or spiritual gifts

-a person holds on to unforgiveness to the offender who has tragically hurt them beyond belief

By now, you may be thinking, "What do the previous examples have to do with "worshiping an idol?" Glance back at verse 18: It speaks of "the *maker* of its mold trusting in it." This tells me we can manufacture (make) idols by believing a "lie" (vs. 18), and by putting our trust in these areas that we look to in order to find fulfillment.

Author Elyse M. Fitzpatrick, says it like this: "Idols aren't just stone statues. No, idols are the thoughts, desires, longings, and expectations that we worship in the place of the true God. Idols cause us to ignore the true God in search of what we think we need."

*After reading Mrs Fitzpatrick's view on idols, are you better able to identify any idols you have constructed in your own mind?

-If so, explain why this is an idol.

*Write out Habakkuk 2:20 below. Read 1 Thessalonians 1:9. How do these verses coupled together serve to remind us of how we can overcome our own personal idol worship?

Repentance means that we not only turn away from something; we must replace what we are turning away from with something else......more specifically, with *Someone* else! God reminds us that He is in His holy temple; He is the one true God! All of our idols will inevitably let us down, wear us out, and leave us wanting. Only Jehovah can fill the void in our lives which we are seeking to fill with other things. All these "things" are based on a lie. Like the Thessalonians, we too, can have the testimony that we have made the choice to turn from useless idols to serve the Living God.

And we can keep on turning to Him, as He continues to reveal areas in our lives where we have set up idols that we may not have realized as such. As one preacher I know says, "Our life is a continual repentance." Because God is in His holy temple we can come before Him and repent.

*Please read Hebrews 4:16, as we close out this week. Spend some time with Jesus asking Him to reveal any idols in your life. Repent of them and ask God to replace the idols in your heart with more of Himself! Your God, who is in His holy temple, on His throne of grace, desires to lavish you with mercy and grace!!!

*Sharing Your Thoughts: What spoke to you most this week and why?

**Please write out your *Week 3 Principle.*

Week 4

Focal Passage:

Habakkuk 3:1-19

Week 4: Day 1

Well! Here we are ladies.....We've come to our last week of study! I always have mixed feelings when we get to this point. I'm encouraged about what we've been learning together and our commitment to come this far. Yet, there's a kind of melancholy feeling knowing we are about to wind it down.

*What about you? What are your thoughts and feelings as we are drawing near to the end of our study?

Of the three chapters we have to choose from in the Book of Habakkuk, this is definitely my favorite. I think you might agree with me by the time we finish up this week.

*So let's get going! Please read Habakkuk 3:1-5.

-What emotion is Habakkuk experiencing as he begins his prayer?

-What is his request in verse 2?

I remember years ago someone telling me that the Bible says, "God came from Teman." This person was apparently quoting from Habakkuk, although at the time I had no clue. However, I think this man was a bit confused. If I understood him correctly, this well-meaning guy was trying to make verse 3 out to mean that God originated somewhere. And that somewhere, was Teman.

It is believed that Teman was a city East of Israel and was the home of one of Job's friends.

*How does 1 Kings 8:27 clear up my friend's misinformed notion that God literally came from, or originated, in Teman?

Scholars believe that today's text, in referring to Teman, indicates God being revealed from the South. Since He is God He can originate His work from any area He chooses.

Habakkuk continues on, by rehearsing God's display of power on behalf of His people as He delivered them from Egyptian bondage.

The prophet is once again speaking to God in prayer, asking Him to revive His magnificent works. Next he begins to recap what some of His works have been. Through Habakkuk's example we can learn how to feed our own faith when it feels like it is floundering.

*Consider the following:

1. Habakkuk, again, poured out his honest feelings before God. He didn't try to come across as staunch and pious. He didn't think, "I'm a prophet so I've got to understand all this and have my act together." Nope! Not Habakkuk! He humbly admits to God that he is afraid. (vs 2)

*How does Psalm 145:18 indicate we are to call upon God?

Habakkuk was sharing his true feelings with his God. That's what we do in close relationships. We know we can trust the person who is listening; therefore, we feel the permission to be open and vulnerable.

So Sisters, when we don't understand what God is doing, when we are confused and afraid, like Habakkuk, we can be open before Him. He wants an intimate love relationship with us. God likes realness! And we might as well be honest about our feelings. He knows them all anyway.

2. Next, after acknowledging his fear, the prophet makes his request. He is asking God for revival. When God revives His works, our heart is also part of His plan.

*What does Isaiah 57:15 say is the prerequisite for having our hearts revived by God?

-When is the last time you have asked God to revive your heart? Are you willing to ask Him today to begin a revival within you?

3 Now, we see Habakkuk beginning to rehearse God's work in the past. It's been said that when we recount God's faithfulness we are feeding our faith. And since God had already told His prophet, "the just shall live by faith," a faith feeding is just what he needed. When we're afraid and struggling it's what we need too.

*How does Psalm 77:9-14 relate the importance of remembering the great works God has done?

*As we close out today I want to encourage you to set aside some time to follow Habakkuk's example.

-What is the most pressing problem, burden, or trial you are facing at this time? Begin by going to your Father in prayer, telling him your honest feelings (fear, doubt, discouragement)

-Next, ask Him to revive your heart that He would become the greatest love of your life, and that He would give you the desire to know and serve Him better.

-Close out by writing in a journal or on an index card (to keep as a reminder) several of the ways God has worked on your behalf in the past. Praise Him, as you recount His mighty works in your personal life. Finally, consider continuing a faithfulness journal so that you can add to it in the future, referring back to it when your faith needs feeding.

Remembering what the Lord has done for you, and what He's doing in you, will boost your faith exponentially! It will help reframe the burden or trial you are currently facing with a reminder of God's constant faithfulness!

Here's our fourth and final principle.

Week 4 Principle: "We ***embrace*** God when we choose to find our joy in Him, rather than our circumstances!"

*Sharing Your Thoughts: How can following Habakkuk's example encourage you in whatever it is you are facing today?

Week 4: Day 2

Yesterday we looked at the example Habakkuk gave us as he lifted up his prayer to God.

*By way of review, please glance back at yesterday's content and list briefly the three elements in Habakkuk's "faith feeding" prayer.

1.

2.

3.

Habakkuk shared his honest feelings with God, he asked God to revive His works, and he began to pray back to God some of His righteous acts in the life of His people, Israel. Today we will read Habakkuk's continuing discourse as he acknowledged God's mighty power.

*Please read Habakkuk 3:6-11. Let's zero in on the last sentence in verse 6. Please write it out below.

Most translations state, "His ways are everlasting." Few things we find ourselves involved in are everlasting. We get excited when our choice of teams wins a championship, yet in all the excitement, this is only temporal. We may spend our life seeking to get ahead and move up the corporate ladder. Yet, none of this will last forever.

But, isn't that what our hearts long for? Isn't that why we love fairy tale endings… "and they lived happily ever after?" Isn't that why we treasure our *keepsake* items, because we want to *keep* them forever? And, isn't this why we use the abbreviation BFF? It's not enough to say we're best friends….we must add the "forever" part.

I've heard it said we were created for eternity. As Habakkuk aptly states, "His (God's) ways are eternal." When we belong to Him our lives have value and count past our fleeting tenure on this earth.

*How does Ecclesiastes 3:11 convey this point?

As I think of the myriad things I do every day that consume my time I have to step back and ask myself, "What, if any, of these things will count for eternity?"

In order for us to ponder over this question, let's shed some light upon it from the pages of God's *everlasting* Word.

*Note beside each verse what is eternal:

-Psalm 119:89 -Romans

8:11

-Psalm 145:13 -Revelation

5:8

-Daniel 12:2

From the above verses we can see that God's kingdom is eternal, as well as people's souls, His Word, and our prayers. Scholars seem to agree, according to Revelation 5:8, that our prayers don't just drift out into a spiritual "cyberspace." God actually keeps them. Since the scene in Revelation is before His throne, I think we can rightly conclude our prayers have eternal value.

*Please share some specific ways of how you can be involved in the following eternal investments:

1. People/souls:

2. God's Word:

3. Prayer:

4. God's kingdom

As Habakkuk recognized how great and eternal God's ways are, so should we! Remember, dear Sisters, we serve an everlasting God who takes the ways we serve Him on this earth and causes them to have eternal value!

*Sharing Your Thoughts: Of the ideas you shared above, which stands out the most to you, and how will you implement it into your daily walk with God?

Week 4: Day 3

As we continue to read Habakkuk's declaration of God's powerful and awesome works, I want us to again focus on the last verse in our passage today. Since we are obviously not as familiar with Hebrew history as Habakkuk was, we may struggle to relate. But something tells me verse 16 is going to resonate with you; it certainly does with me.

*Please read Habakkuk 3:12-16

-If you had to use only one word to describe Habakkkuk's mental and emotional state in verse 16, what would it be?

I'd love to hear your answers, and I wonder if any of you wrote the word I did: Dread! That's what I sense the prophet is experiencing, along with fear. These emotions often go hand in hand.

Most likely, we've all experienced these unwanted feelings at one time or another in our life. We equate them with angst and a sense of impending doom.

*According to verse 16, in what ways does Habakkuk describe the physical effects fear is causing in his body?

I've got to say it again: I just love this guy, because I'm attracted to real and vulnerable people. I think maybe God is too! Think about it! The Lord could have kept Habakkuk's weak and struggling vulnerabilities out of His Holy Word if He wanted to. Aren't you so glad He didn't? In fact, Habakkuk is just one, among many of God's people whom He allows us to be privy to their struggles and brokenness. Let's consider a few more.

*Please read the following verses, recording beside each one the name of the person and how they described their plight.

-1 Kings 19:2-4

-Job 3:26 (the name of the Book just might give this character's name away)

-1 Corinthians 2:3

-Finally, read the Words Jesus shared with His followers in The Garden of Gethsemane (Matthew 26:37-38). How did Jesus convey His feelings?

Somehow we get the idea in order to follow Christ we have to appear strong and resilient to those watching. God chose to include, in His Holy Word, glimpses of people who loved and served Him, yet wrestled through doubt, discouragement, fear, and sorrow. The fact that God allows us to see this among His followers really encourages me. It frees me up to be ok with being broken and needy, joining myriad other people who loved God, yet also struggled amidst life's uncertainties.

Even Jesus, being fully God, but also fully man, allowed His disciples to see the extent of His soul's sorrow as He faced His last hours before the cross. Since God has the prerogative, He could have chosen to keep Jesus' heartfelt emotions out of Scripture. He could have let that stay between Christ and His followers. But instead, He has allowed every Bible reader since then to "look in" on this poignant time in our Savior's life.

*Why do you think God allows us to see such candid pictures of His people in Scripture? How can this affect your own life?

The next two days will exude a great turn around in the life of the prophet we've come to know and love! I'm anticipating for us to culminate our study together as we see the work God has been doing in Habakkuk's heart all along!

*Sharing Your Thoughts: How did the people we read about today help you in your quest to accept your weaknesses, while being real and open before your God?

Week 4: Day 4

This morning, while I was continuing to work through Kelly Minter's study, "Finding God Faithful," Kelly recapped the faithful lovingkindness of the Lord to Joseph and his family. I sensed God reminding me of His constant faithfulness to me. I, too, have experienced His mercy, forgiveness, redemption, and grace in my life, time and time again.

As I look back over my walk with Christ there are times when I stood on the mountaintop and basked in God's goodness, feeling like I would never be moved from that place of peace and abundance. And, there's been other times when I felt I was so far down in the valley, so hopeless and helpless, I believed I'd never see the light of day. I thought I would never again experience the joy of the Lord, or His peaceful presence in my life. But I was wrong!

What I'm coming to realize through all of life's ups and downs is that I have absolutely no reason to put any confidence in myself; instead my hope and endurance comes in knowing Jesus is my only safe place and my only sure "thing."

*What about you? During your tenure of walking with Jesus, describe below your own personal experiences:

1. What has been your highest mountaintop experience with Jesus?

2. What has been your lowest valley in your walk of faith?

3. What did you learn from both of these experiences?

I love the mountaintops. I'm guessing you do too. It's so easy to praise God when all seems right with the world, and especially in our own little personal worlds! God does indeed afford us seasons of ecstatic joy, but if we're being honest these are not the times that call for a huge amount of faith. When everything appears to be going well we really don't have to place our complete and surrendered trust in God, do we? It is then we walk with eyes of sight.

That's one reason we will continue to have seasons that challenge our faith as we travel the dusty soil of planet earth; for our faith to grow and be strengthened, it must be tested. Habakkuk, the prophet, who was literally shaking in his shoes with fear in the verse we read yesterday, has done an about face in our text today. Can't wait for you to see the apex of our study!

*Please turn to Habakkuk 3:17-18 (pick up in verse 16 just so you can appreciate such a radical change.)

*How would you describe Habakkuk's amazing turnaround?

Produce and livestock provided many of the basic human needs during Habakkuk's days. There wasn't a Walmart on every corner; folks depended on God's provision by working with the basic elements of the land. The impending danger of the invading Chaldeans would change Israel's bounty, causing the provisions they depended on to not be taken for granted.

Think back over the covid pandemic, our current state of shortages with certain items, and the concern of a recession. People panic as these pertinent issues bring chaos to our land. Habakkuk's concern was even greater; having a shortage of food and other necessities needed for survival, while their enemies would wreak havoc as they marched through their land.

Yet, this fearful man whom we've just seen scared out of his wits, renews his focus. He opts to place his perspective, not on the possible lack of "essentials," but on his one and only hope, His

Essential God. Habakkuk moved from operating in fear to making a choice to take his next steps in faith. His faith convicts me and challenges me!

*How are you convicted by the choice Habakkuk made?

-How are you challenged by it?

Please observe that God had not changed Habakkuk's circumstances, nor His plan for bringing judgment on the nation of Israel. The change God made was in the heart of His child who chose to bring his honest doubts and questions to Him. During the process of his struggles, Habakkuk's faith was stretched and challenged. Therefore, it grew in the process. Wrestling with our faith is not necessarily a bad thing if we wrestle toward God and not away from Him!

Habakkuk's testimony encourages us, causing us to recognize that no matter how the future looks, we can put our focus back on Christ and choose to rejoice in Him.

Habakkuk made a fresh proclamation of faith. He had decided no matter how bad things appeared, his true life was found in God; in Him alone he would find his joy. Now it's time for us to make a fresh proclamation of faith ourselves. Certainly, the big world around us looks like it's facing God's judgment. The signs of the times are all around. And besides that, most of the folks I know are facing their own personal crisis in one way or another.

Our times, like Habakkuk's, may only get harder. But, we too have a choice. We can remain stuck, shaking in our shoes, and facing each new day with fear. Or we can choose to stay in fellowship with God, bringing our fears and doubts to Him, and choosing the joy that comes from a relationship with Christ, rather than a happiness that depends on our circumstances.

*Please write down the four greatest fears, worries, or concerns that are challenging you at the present time. (national or personal)

1.

2.

3.

4.

*How are you dealing with these hardships in your own way?

-How is this working out for you?

-What if you sought the Lord's joy in spite of each hardship?

-What if you really believed that with every single heartbreaking devastation you will ever face, Jesus will be right beside you?

-What if you trusted Jesus enough to believe He will work through your pain and sorrow and use it for good?

-What if you believed His joy will ultimately triumph in your life?

*What assurance does Psalm 30:5 give us?

-Following Habakkuk's example in Chapter 3:17-18, consider writing out your own proclamation of faith in the space below. Transfer it to your journal or on a notecard, telling God you will make the choice to look to Him for joy!

*Sharing Your Thoughts: What is your greatest challenge in choosing joy for your life today? What is one step you can take to help you make the crucial journey toward joy?

Week 4: Day 5

Ladies, as we conclude our last day of study we have only one more verse to read in this short, three chapter Book that bears our, now familiar, prophet's name.

*Please read Habakkuk 3:19.

-What does Habakkuk conclude about:

God?

Himself?

His circumstances?

Habakkuk was instructed by God in Chapter One that the just person shall live by his faith. Then as it happens in the life of every believer, the prophet moves from God's classroom to His field trip. This is where he learns, "hands on," what the walk of faith is all about.

Habakkuk learned true faith in Jehovah shines the brightest when times are the darkest. Nothing in the prophets' circumstances had changed; the dreadful future events God had proclaimed would still take place.

What did change was Habakkuk's heart and mind. He came to realize with a deep rooted confidence that God was his strength. He would give the prophet feet like those of the deer to tread upon the high hills he would have to climb.

*What is your “high hill” that you need God’s strength to climb today in your life?

-Has your “high hill” changed any since we began this study?

-How has what we have learned thus far encouraged you for the future hills you may have to scale?

The NKJV translates the latter part of verse nine as, “He will make me walk on my high hills.” Although I know high heel shoes were not the fashion trend during Habakkuk’s time (and if they were I think it’s safe to say he wouldn’t be wearing them), I want to chuckle when I read this phrase.

For those of us women who still try to wear high heels, we know how uncomfortable, awkward, and downright painful they can become after too long of a walk in them.....especially uphill! It’s the same in our spiritual walk; when we feel each day is an uphill battle, we get tired and want to quit.

Only faith in Jesus Christ, the One True Living God, enables us to not only make the ascent, but actually move ahead with faith, hope, and yes, even joy in our uphill battles. How did that work in Habakkuk’s life and how can we incorporate it into our own?

*Please look back at verse 19. Habakkuk begins this final verse by focusing on the Lord. Some translations of this verse begin with, “The Sovereign Lord........”

-What does the fact that God is sovereign mean to you?

God is the Supreme Being in total control over the universe He has created, as well as everything in it. I believe over the course of Habakkuk's struggle, the idea of who God really is grew exponentially. And as it did, his faith grew with it.

Habakkuk learned the value of renewing his mind to focus on God instead of his circumstances. When he was treading those high hills he had to climb, he chose to move his mind upward as well!

Since we know the battle is primarily for our mind, it is here that we faint and flounder, or choose to be renewed and revived.

*According to Romans 12:2, what are God's instructions to His children?

Renewing our mind is a battle, but it can be done. If not, God would have never told us to do it. Every time we choose to stand on God's Word, every time we replace the negative and destructive thoughts the enemy sends our way with God's Truth, we are renewing our minds!

Habakkuk's story ensures us that winning this battle is possible; it's also more than worth the fight. And thankfully, we don't fight on our own. Our relationship with Jesus is what assures us we will finish well! He's already embracing us; we need to open up our hearts, and embrace Him back. It's my opinion that Jesus loves a big ole bear hug from His children! Remember the prophet's name means "embrace." Our protagonist truly learned the joy and peace that comes from embracing his God. I hope we are learning it too!

*How do the following verses help us to understand that when we choose to embrace God, He is already embracing us, waiting for our response?

-Deuteronomy 33:27

-Jeremiah 31:3

-Matthew 11:28

From the Old Testament to the New, God is drawing and embracing those who answer His invitation to salvation, and to those who long to grow closer to Him. Regardless of what our past has been, or what our future holds, what great assurance we have in Jesus!!! When life knocks us down, when the future looks uncertain, and even if we're so afraid our knees are knocking like Habakkuk's were, we have an open invitation to bask in the presence of Jesus! We can leave behind our fear and despair and embrace the One Who longs to comfort us in His mighty arms!

*As we prepare to wrap up our study, please read Paul's encouraging words in Philippians 3:12-14.

-What was Paul committed to doing? Note everything you observe.

Like Paul, Habakkuk also chose to take the high road! He didn't allow the hardships of life to hold him down. He moved on past his fears and set his feet on the upward path; those "high hills" he would have to climb. But with each step he walked in faith, he moved ever closer to his God. I'm reminded of a quote I read by Hannah Whitall Smith: "Every trial and hardship is just a chariot to take us to a higher place with God, but we go on the wings of trust and surrender."

So embrace Jesus in your chariot, Sisters! For He is ever embracing you!

*Sharing Your Thoughts: What is your biggest takeaway from the Book of Habakkuk? How will it make a difference in your walk of faith?

*Please write out your *Week 4 Principle.* Then conclude your study by reviewing and writing all four weekly principles in the next section.

My Weekly Principals

Week 1 Principle:

Week 2 Principle:

Week 3 Principle:

Week 4 Principle

A note to my readers: I hope you have enjoyed getting to know Habakkuk as much as I have! My heart's desire, more than anything else, is that you feel you have gotten to know your God in a more intimate way.

I pray that our journey of faith will take us day by day into a closer walk with Jesus. And, when our feet finally touch down on those streets of gold, we will stand before Him and embrace Him like we never have before!

Appendix: How to know I am a Christian.

The very basis of our faith begins with being assured that we know Jesus and will spend eternity with Him! Salvation has been described as a two-sided coin. One side is the faith side and the other side is the repentance side.

When we realize we are a sinner in need of a Savior, we can turn to Jesus Christ, the one true God who died on the cross to forgive us of our sins and make the way for us to have a relationship with Him. If we're willing to place our FAITH in His death, burial, and resurrection on our personal behalf and to call out to Him for salvation, He assures us that He will save us! (Romans 10:13).

The flip side of the coin is included in this decision. It happens when we REPENT. We must be willing to not only place our faith in Him, but also to allow Him to change us. We must turn from our sins and turn to Jesus. When we have repented and placed our faith in Christ alone, we are assured we will have eternal life with Him in heaven. We also will now have His Holy Spirit residing within us to help us grow in our Christian life.

Being baptized, becoming involved in a Bible-believing church, being discipled through His Word, and fellowshipping with other believers are important ways to live out your faith as a new believer. If you have just given your life to Jesus Christ, Congratulations! Please share this great news with a local pastor or trusted Christian friend! They can help you to take the next step of faith on your life long journey to know Christ more!

I would also love to hear how God has spoken to you during your journey through the Book of Habakkuk? Please feel free to email me at busywomensstudy@yahoo.com. I appreciate you, Sisters, more than you know!

The Busy Women's Bible Study Series

Thank you again, dear Sisters, for joining me for the Busy Women's Bible Study Series. Please look for more studies in this series to come! Blessings and much love, Mary

busywomensstudy@yahoo.com

Made in the USA
Columbia, SC
04 December 2024